KUBSIM:
A SIMULATION IN COLLECTIVE BARGAINING

KUBSIM:
A SIMULATION IN COLLECTIVE BARGAINING
Second Edition

By

Lawrence A. Klatt
Florida Atlantic University

and

Thomas F. Urban
Texas A & M University

 Grid Publishing, Inc.

Printed in the United States of America.

I.S.B.N. 0-88244-245-7

Printing 10 9 8 7 6 5 4 3 2

Library of Congress Cataloging in Publication Data

Klatt, Lawrence A.
     KUBSIM, a simulation in collective bargaining.

     (Grid series in management)
     1. Collective bargaining—Study and teaching—
Simulation methods. 2. Simulation games in
education.

I. Urban, Thomas F. II. Title. III. Series.
HD6971.5.K55 1981   658.3'154   81-7153
ISBN 0-88244-245-7 (pbk.)

TABLE OF CONTENTS

ACKNOWLEDGEMENTS

The authors are indebted to the following people for their assistance in this revised edition.

1. James A. Beier
   Earlham College

2. Frank Bowen
   Defiance College

3. Steven S. Briggs
   California State University, Long Beach

4. Newton Ellis
   Texas A & M University

5. Mildren Fox
   Texas A & M University

6. Myron Gable
   Shippensburg State College

7. Vern E. Hauck
   University of Alaska, Anchorage

8. Melvin Kleeblatt
   Florida Atlantic University

9. Anthony Redwood
   University of Kansas

INTRODUCTION

Experience strongly indicates that greater student interest in assigned reading material and increased classroom participation is achieved when theoretical concepts are related to practical situations. Research in the area of learning theory reinforces this contention. Such is the case in courses dealing with labor relations.

Over the years, the authors discovered that the typical lecture-textbook approach falls short of meeting the expectations of both student and instructor. Students often find the somewhat theoretical issues, concepts, and ideas in most labor-management courses too abstract or at least difficult to relate to the dynamic process of collective bargaining. It became apparent that increased student participation is necessary and that a case-type approach might be the solution to the problem.

While cases offered the student the opportunity to apply theories or broad generalizations to a specific set of facts, the case approach had limitations. The static nature of a case minimized the importance of considering facts in relation to an existing power structure, given roles and personalities, and the realistic pressures of time. To overcome some of these limitations, role playing in connection with the case method was introduced. Ultimately, the authors devised a "living case" or, as it is more fashionably called, "simulations of a competitive nature"--an experiential approach to labor relations.

Thus, KUBSIM, besides affording the player an opportunity to apply lecture or text material, provides the opportunity to make decisions which have real consequences on the ultimate outcome. Furthermore, without the pressures of real-life losses, the player is encouraged to utilize innovative strategies and tactics to the resolution of conflict situations. Finally, since events and time are telescoped, actual conflict situations develop, resources become scarce, trade-offs are required, and compromise strategies developed through a team consensus are both possible and necessary.

Continuing with the progression of events, the performance audit of each negotiating team serves a multiplicity of purposes. Learning theory stresses feedback and knowledge of results. Thus for the team members, it provides the feedback for the question of "How did we do?" In our experience with the audit, we have assigned teams who negotiated as unions to audit management groups and vice versa. In this respect, it enables each student in the course to see both sides of the picture--union and management. In addition, the audit as well as the information generated throughout the negotiation enables the instructor to objectively evaluate the performance of each team and team member.

OBJECTIVES AND DESCRIPTIONS

KUBSIM is a collective bargaining simulation developed to familiarize the participants with the bargaining issues, strategies, and pressures involved in union-management relationships. It combines the political, as well as the economic, forces at work and illustrates the necessity for careful consideration to the ramifications of negotiated issues. It is not designed to "teach bargaining" as such, but rather to give the student a practical approach to the strategy and substantive information required in contract negotiation and administration. KUBSIM is designed to complement alternative teaching styles. It enables students to experience the dynamics of collective bargaining.

As a player in KUBSIM, you will be a member of either the union or management negotiating team. The goal of your team will be to negotiate an agreement on demands which it believes to be most important. You will negotiate such "real-life" issues as wages, vacations, union security, seniority, management rights, and sub-contracting. In the sections on "KUBSIM Industries" and "Union-Management Relations at KUB," your team receives statements of its perspective and outlook on certain important issues.

The Role Descriptions on pages 21 to 31 describe personal positions on various bargaining issues. These descriptions are not intended to stifle or confine your activities or ingenuity. Rather they will assist you in identifying with a specific member of an actual negotiation team, and enable each team to delegate and provide for descriptions for each member of the team. This allows for some degree of specialization to develop among you and your teammates--a helpful development for facilitating research, material collection, and strategy formulation.

Through participation in these simulation exercises, you will be exposed to all phases of the collective bargaining process: studying the position of both management and the union; gathering facts and information; formulating a strategy and appropriate tactics to carry out the strategy; negotiating the contract; meeting in caucuses for in-depth discussions of issues; and, critiquing the final results. Lastly, you will settle a series of conflicts arising out of the contract you negotiated. In short, you will have "experienced" what collective bargaining is "all about"--at least, until you begin to play for "real chips."

GROUND RULES

1. No extension of the existing contract will be permitted. At the conclusion of the bargaining, each chairman must hand in Form F describing the final agreement or, if no agreement, the team's final proposal. Clauses which refer a demand to a post-negotiation committee should not be negotiated.

2. Absolutely no consultation with any of the other team(s), regardless of company or union, will be permitted prior to bargaining sessions.

3. The chairman of each team (the President of Local 305 and the Director - Corporate Industrial Relations) will coordinate the planning and strategy sessions, and coordinate work assignments with team members. The chairman should also coordinate but not monopolize actual negotiations. Each member of the team should play an active role in the sessions.

4. Someone on each team should keep track of settlements. There is no immediate need to write out the contract clauses in detail. Be sure, however, to record the essential substance of the agreement.

5. Each team will develop and present no less than six demands (or contract changes) and not more than ten. All demands must be based on the facts in the case. (All aspects of a wage demand, e.g., across-the-board, cost of living, etc., will count as one demand. Fringe benefits, if demanded, will count as a separate demand.)

6. Each participant will engage in necessary research for the negotiation. Potential sources for research are available through library, governmental, and other facilities.

7. The "initial demand" or "lowest acceptable offer" need not bind a team in actual negotiations. But a team should make its anticipated limits as realistic as possible.

8. Each team should keep all its materials in a manila folder in order to supply the audit team with evaluative information.

EXHIBIT I

PROCEDURE SUMMARY

MEETING	PURPOSE	SUMMARY	SUGGESTED # OF CLASS SESSIONS (1 HOUR CLASS)
1 (Group)	Introduction to KUBSIM	A. Assignment of Union and Management Teams B. Assignment of Roles C. Review of Ground Rules D. Discussion of Availability of Resource Materials	1

2 (Separate) May be held outside of classroom setting	Planning and Strategy Sessions	A. Discuss and analyze simulation among teammates; develop role descriptions
		B. Conduct necessary research to develop bargaining priorities, proposals, and positions
		C. Present proposals based upon role descriptions
		D. Formulate Strategy Format (Form A)
		  1. Establish a priority of demands
		  2. For each item demanded, establish lowest acceptable offer; initial demand offer; expectation of final agreement
		E. Develop a Bargaining Agenda (Form B)
		F. Develop an Argumentation Sequence (Form C) for Demands: Develop order of presentation; who will handle the negotiating for each item (resource); list argument in favor of demand as well as anticipated rebuttal
		G. Prepare a Rebuttal Schedule (Form D): Anticipate the demands of opponents; estimate the priorities of their demands; estimate the initial demand expectations; who will handle the rebuttal; what evidence will you give in refuting the demands
			2 – 5

4

EXHIBIT I
(continued)

MEETING	PURPOSE	SUMMARY	SUGGESTED # OF CLASS SESSIONS (1 HOUR CLASS)
3	Contract Bargaining Sessions	A. Exchange at least two copies of Form B B. Introduce members of each team and formulate any additional ground rules C. Teams present brief verbal justification for each demand D. Meet in caucus to discuss opponents' demands E. Develop possible compromises, counter-proposals, and trade-offs in light of opponents' and your demands F. Negotiate G. Concur H. Settle or Strike!	3
4	Wrap-up Session for Negotiations	A. Chairmen present summary of agreement to remainder of class (Form F) B. Instructor's comments on overall negotiations	1
5	Audit Preparation	A. Each team prepares evaluation of opposing team (Form G) B. Assignment of audit groups C. Audit groups evaluate contracts (Forms H & I)	2 - 4
6	Audit Presentation	A. Audit presentation B. Individual appraisal (Form J)	1

Note: Sessions 4, 5, and 6 may be telescoped depending upon time availability.

5

KUB INDUSTRIES

One day in 1960 Tom Ruban contacted an old college buddy, Larry Kraft, to invite him to join in a business venture. After much investigation and analysis, the two men decided to pool their savings to purchase a marginal, poorly managed machine shop which the owner was very anxious to sell. The business was located in a city of 45,000 people situated about 45 miles from Detroit. The two men decided that the future of their business was to be found in tapping the special order business from the many firms in the area which were engaged in auto parts manufacturing. As a result of an intensive order solicitation campaign, the two men were able to obtain several lucrative orders from parts manufacturers located within a 50-mile radius. The firm continued to grow and by the end of 1962, it was employing 10 full-time employees and one part-time employee in addition to the two partners.

Midway through 1964, the partners obtained a large government contract to manufacture parts for government vehicles. In order to raise the funds necessary to expand their business to handle this large contract, the partners incorporated under the name of KUB Industries with 5,000 shares of common stock. The partners kept 2,600 shares for themselves, sold 1,000 shares to three employees, and the balance of 1,400 shares went to a venture capital group located in the Detroit area. Government loans and guarantees were generously used to expand the plant and acquire much of the needed equipment. With the assistance of the local employment office, the firm was able to locate and train the additional 200 people needed to operate the expanded operations.

The firm continued to grow rapidly in terms of sales and manpower. By the end of 1967, sales amounted to $28 million and the labor force reached a new high of 700 employees. From 1967 until 1970, KUB Industries faced some serious problems as it attempted to readjust to a slower pace. The loss of government contracts was a severe blow to company sales and profits. As a result, employment at KUB Industries in 1970 was only 70 percent of its peak 1967 total. Fortunately, due to the growth of the auto industry and the company's proximity to the major auto firms, KUB Industries was able to make a successful transition to the manufacturing of auto parts. In fact, by the end of 1973, KUB was employing 950 workers with sales totaling over $58 million. From 1974 to 1978, sales reached a high of over $71 million, with net profts after taxes showing a good return on invested capital. (See Tables I, II, and III for a summary of financial data.) Sales fell in 1979, due to the loss of a sizeable contract with a parts dealer. As a result of the downturn in domestic auto sales, 1980 sales were substantially below projections.

In the early part of 1981, the KUB management team gathered in an executive meeting to analyze the 1980 financial data and to review plans for the next several years. Mr. Ruban, the president, pointed out that the company was now heavily dependent on the auto industry, with slightly over 60 percent of sales going to the four domestic auto manufacturers and another 20 percent going to auto repair and auto parts dealers. Government contract work accounted for the balance of sales or just about 20 percent. The firm's product line now included fan belts, radiators, heaters, carburetors, ball joints, and piston rings. Mr. Ruban was also concerned about the future outlook for the automotive industry. He re-emphasized the point that KUB Industries was heavily dependent on domestic auto sales, which were depressed during the latter part of 1979, 1980, and the first part of 1981.

In fact, he cited several industry reports that projected a continual dismal outlook for 1981 domestic auto sales. The cause of this reduction in new car sales was held to be due to several factors, one of which was the failure of the major domestic producers to anticipate the shift in consumer demand to smaller, more economical cars. This was evidenced by the fact that, while U. S. producers were losing sales in record proportions, the larger producers of foreign economy cars had posted record sales for 1980. Other reasons for low auto sales were the rising cost of gasoline, an uncertain economic outlook, and higher interest rates.

The combined effect of the current economic factors was causing consumers to hold and repair their cars rather than trade them in for new ones. Mr. Kraft, the executive vice president, cited one study which showed that the average age of cars on the road had increased from 6.0 years in 1975 to 6.5 years in 1980. This, combined with the increasing total number of motor vehicles in use, virtually assured a long-term uptrend in sales of replacement parts.

In order to diversify and to reduce dependence on the slipping sales of the major domestic producers, KUB was considering several options. One part of their long term strategy was to increase sales efforts in the area of replacement parts for used cars, commonly known as "aftermarket" parts. This is an extremely competitive market and the KUB management was well aware that every opportunity to conserve labor costs through automation or other innovative production methods would have to be utilized. Along these lines, plans called for the company to invest approximately $5.5 million in new, automated equipment which would substantially increase production capacity while decreasing the need for semi-skilled and unskilled labor. The expansion would be primarily financed through retained earnings and a loan for $2 million from the Citizens Bank of Detroit. While the modernization program was expected to reduce the need for semi-skilled and unskilled labor by about 17 percent, the new equipment would require an increase of about 6 percent in the skilled ranks. Mr. Ruban re-emphasized the point that the competitive nature of the auto parts industry along with recent technological advances made it imperative that the firm undergo the modernization program.

During 1978, the company was working at capacity to provide parts to the auto industry which was enjoying a boom period. This resulted in an average of eight hours per week of overtime for each of the firm's 1,200 hourly employees during the year. Since the government contract work was sporadic and frequently called for special skill requirements, overtime work could not be evenly distributed. In fact, a large group of employees worked 54 hours a week throughout most of 1978 and the first part of 1979. While the labor contract gives management the right to require overtime and to select who shall work overtime, about 75 employees who had been averaging 54-hour work weeks refused to continue working overtime. Under the threat of dismissal they finally consented to work. During the past year, as management has attempted to bring production in line with slumping sales, overtime has become very limited. Now, a large number of employees have been complaining that the foremen have shown favoritism in selecting who shall have the right to earn extra money by working overtime.

Even with the increased overtime, KUB had found it necessary from time to time to sub-contract out the assembly of some parts. During the period 1978-80, the subcontracted assembly work amounted to only 4 percent of total sales. At the same time, a small but growing amount of skilled work has been subcontracted out. The company has maintained that this is within their management prerogatives and furthermore is necessary to remain competitive and meet contract deadlines during peak demand periods. The workers have complained that the subcontracting has been done to get "cheap" labor from non-unionized firms located in the South.

As Mr. Ruban sat in his office contemplating the forthcoming union–management negotiations, he was momentarily relieved to receive a "report" via the grapevine that the financial reserves of the local union could not support a strike of any duration. He was already aware that a recent, lengthy strike against a large firm in the industry had seriously depleted the strike funds of the International Union. He knew that a strike at this time against KUB Industries would have disastrous consequences for the company.

UNION-MANAGEMENT RELATIONS AT KUB INDUSTRIES

Background

During the early history of the company, several unions had attempted to organize the workers. It was not until late in 1970, however, that Local 305 of the International Union won a representation election by a small margin at KUB Industries. Prior to this time, KUB had a reputation in the community of being a good place to work. This attitude was perpetuated by progressive management practices and better than average wages. In 1970, however, the loss of government contracts and the resulting mass layoffs created worker discontent and provided the nucleus for a successful organization drive.

The negotiations following the union vote resulted in a bitter strike when the company refused to allow the union's demands for a union shop and union participation in transfers, layoffs, and certain work rules. After a six-week strike, the workers returned to work with a three-year contract when management agreed to the union shop. Ever since the 1970 strike, the relationship between management and the workers has never been the same. While all subsequent negotiations have taken place without a strike, only some last-minute concessions by management have avoided a strike during the last two contract negotiations.

About three months ago a "wildcat strike" took place in the Finishing Department with the alleged reason being discriminatory practices on the part of two white foremen. The young, minority workers in the department accused the foremen of assigning them the dirty work and of giving preferential treatment to the white workers with regard to transfers and vacation assignments. No employees were disciplined because of the strike and management felt that satisfactory progress had been made in easing tension in the department. However, several recent machine breakdowns have been traced to acts of sabotage and evidence exists which implicates a group of militants in at least one case.

Management has sensed a great deal of militancy on the part of the union since the last negotiations. It is believed that this has been brought about by four principal factors:

(1) The presence of many more younger workers in the union;

(2) The knowledge that management is embarking on a vast modernization plan which is likely to result in substantial transfers and layoffs;

(3) Another international union has been trying to win over the KUB employees;

(4) Growing economic uncertainty and union concern over eroding real wages and job security.

9

Some of the key elements included in the current contract include:

Wage and Benefits

The company uses local wage rates as the basis for its wage structure. The current average wage for the production workers in the company is $7.78 per hour. There are 120 skilled employees among the 1,200 hourly employees. The skilled employees, who include mechanics, tool and die makers, "technicians," millwrights, plumbers, and electricians, are paid an average straight time rate of $9.08 per hour. The company is set up on a two shift per day basis, five days a week, with the second shift earning an 18 cent per hour premium. All jobs have been evaluated according to the National Metal Trade Association job evaluation method. A basic wage rate exists for each of the 12 job classes. The union has always been "suspicious" of the job evaluation method and has demanded an active role in the evaluation of all new jobs.

The current contract has no provision for cost of living adjustments or annual improvement factors. Both issues were brought up in the last negotiations and are expected to receive a strong push from the union this year. The workers are especially concerned about the erosion of their pay checks due to the rising cost of living. The union has pointed to the existence of both benefits in contracts negotiated with the auto manufacturers.

The current contract has five fringe benefits which cost the company $2.08 cents per hour. These include:

(1) Seven paid holidays - Memorial Day, July 4th, Labor Day, Thanksgiving, Christmas Day, New Year's Day, and President's Day.

(2) From one to three weeks of vacation depending on the employee's length of continuous service with the company.

(3) Pension Plan - 60% contributed by the company; vested after 10 years of service; retirement at 65.

(4) Group medical insurance plan - 60% contributed by the company.

(5) A 15-minute coffee break in the morning and afternoon plus a 30-minute lunch break.

The union has maintained that all these benefits are inadequate and need to be increased. In addition, several vocal groups in the union are pushing for additional benefits. For example, the younger workers feel that prime emphasis in the fringe benefit area should be placed on more vacation time with the employee having the right to choose when to take his vacation. The older workers are pushing for increased retirement benefits including retirement at 60 and 100% contribution by the company. The black employees are demanding an eighth paid holiday on the date commemorating Martin Luther King's birthday. There has also been a lot of talk among workers for getting some kind of dental insurance plan and a guarantee of a half day's pay in the event of machine failure, lack of work, or any other occurrence beyond the worker's control.

Administrative Issues

The last couple of years have been marked by an increase in the number of grievances concerning seniority. The seniority provisions in the current contract are broadly stated and subject to various interpretations. For example, during the most recent layoff, there was considerable disagreement regarding "bumping rights." Some of the problems are illustrated by the following issues raised: Should employees claiming "ability" to perform jobs claimed by bumping rights be given a "trial period" on the new job? If so, what is a reasonable trial period? Similarly, the "recall rights" of senior employees have created serious administrative problems. For example, do recall rights apply only to the specific job from which the worker was separated? How much and what kind of recall notice must be given to a laid-off worker?

Employee turnover at KUB Industries is low relative to similar firms. In fact, one-third of the employees have over 20 years of seniority; another one-third have from 10 to 20 years; and the remaining have less than 10 years (the majority of which are minorities, who were hired within the past year and a half.) The company has always followed a promotion policy based on seniority and ability. Accordingly, seniority becomes the dominant factor when two or more employees have very similar qualifications. Within the past couple of months a militant group of recently hired employees has threatened to bring suit against the company and union. They want the company to immediately install an affirmative action program whereby 15 percent of all higher classified job vacancies will be filled by minorities.

The question of "super-seniority" has been heatedly debated during the last negotiations. The union has maintained that preferred status in the event of layoffs should be given to all union officers, including the 30 shop stewards, regardless of their length of service. Management has felt that special seniority privileges run counter to the seniority concept and in addition are difficult to administer. The militant faction in the union has also made it known that they will not agree to a new contract which does not provide protection against layoffs for the many newly hired minorities. They have maintained that this is necessary to make up for alleged past discriminatory employment practices on the part of management and the union.

While absenteeism has always been somewhat of a problem in the industry, it has become a serious problem at KUB. On several occasions, Monday and Friday absenteeism almost forced the closing of a couple of departments. Management has made it known that in the new contract they want some strong language dealing with absenteeism.

The present contract provides for a grievance procedure and arbitration for contract disputes but it specifically excludes production standards. The company has always argued that the setting of standards is a necessary management right. During the past several months, a substantial number of disputes have occurred over production standards. Management was finally able to negotiate a settlement with the union which proved to be very unpopular with the workers involved. The union feels that production standards will become an even "hotter" issue as management begins its modernization program.

Management has also become concerned about the growing amount of time spent by the stewards on "handling grievances." Many foremen have claimed that the stewards are often just wasting time or discussing union politics with workers rather than discussing legitimate grievances. The company is also concerned about the rise in the number of cases going to arbitration. Since the company pays the full cost of arbitration, management feels that the union is irresponsive to the costs involved and frequently pushes a grievance to arbitration, hoping to get a more favorable settlement. Several foremen have also accused the stewards of manufacturing grievances to instill a sense of militance among the rank and file.

Union Security and Management Rights

The current contract does not contain a "checkoff" provision. The company has opposed collecting dues on philosophical grounds. As a result, the stewards spend considerable time on dues collection during working hours. As part of management's attempt to reduce the time stewards spend supposedly in union business, a notice was recently sent to all stewards and union officials stating that union business, other than the handling of grievances, would not be tolerated on company time.

The management of KUB has always argued that the management of the business in all its phases and details shall remain vested entirely with the employer. Accordingly, the company has refused to allow anything in past contracts which would detract in any way from its right to efficiently operate the business, including issues such as contracting out work, introducing new machinery, setting production standards, or changing job content.

In the past, only a very small amount of assembly work has been subcontracted out. However, during the past year a growing amount of skilled work has been done elsewhere. On two occasions the union had threatened to walk out. Rumor has it that the union wants veto power over all subcontracting work and will demand during the coming negotiations that the company be required to prove to the union that time, expense, or facility restrictions prevent it from allowing present employees to perform the work.

The employees, well aware of the company's modernization program, are quite concerned about the impact of automation on their jobs. Several members of the union's negotiation planning committee have proposed that the next contract require joint labor-management consultation prior to the introduction of any automated change. Other members have proposed special job and wage provisions for down-graded workers to offset any income losses suffered by such workers.

TABLES

TABLE I
KUB Industries – Balance Sheet
1979 and 1980

	1979	1980
Assets		
Cash	$2,940,000	$2,500,000
Accounts receivable, net	9,660,000	9,700,000
Inventories	9,044,000	9,644,000
Prepayments	1,246,000	1,032,000
Total Current Assets	$22,890,000	$22,876,000
Investments	4,536,000	4,024,000
Plant and Equipment, net	27,244,000	27,642,000
Total Assets	$54,670,000	$54,542,000
Liabilities		
Notes payable	$5,502,000	$5,490,000
Accounts payable	3,338,000	3,298,000
Accrued payroll, interest, etc.	4,295,000	4,290,000
Income taxes	784,000	767,000
Total Current Liabilities	$13,919,000	$13,845,000
Long-Term Debt and Reserves	21,371,000	21,260,000
Capital Stock	5,924,000	5,924,000
Retained Earnings	13,456,000	13,513,000
	$54,670,000	$54,542,000

TABLE II
KUB Industries – Statement of Earnings
1979 and 1980

	1979		1980	
Net Sales		$70,607,000		70,400,000
Cost and Expenses				
Cost of sales	63,453,000		63,350,000	
Selling, administrative & general expenses	2,015,000		2,021,000	
Other expenses, net	1,365,000	66,833,000	1,282,000	66,653,000
Earnings before taxes		3,774,000		3,747,000
Taxes		1,304,000		1,160,000
Net earnings		2,470,000		2,587,000

TABLE III
KUB Industries - Net Sales and Earnings
1974 - 1980

Year	Net Sales	Net Earnings
1974	62,400,000	2,472,500
1975	62,041,000	2,312,500
1976	64,050,000	2,750,000
1977	68,125,000	3,042,500
1978	71,790,000	3,202,000
1979	70,607,000	2,470,000
1980	70,400,000	2,587,000
1981*	70,340,100	2,600,000

*Estimated

TABLE IV
Consumer Price Index (All Items)
[1967=100]

		U.S. City Average	Detroit
1981	April	266.8	272.4
	January	260.5	268.5
1980	October	253.9	264.3
	July	247.8	253.7
	April	242.5	248.2
	January	233.2	237.2
1979	October	225.4	227.2
	July	218.9	219.5
	April	211.5	213.2
	January	204.7	205.1
1978	October	200.9	200.9
	July	196.7	194.6
	April	191.5	190.2
	January	187.2	185.0
1977	October	184.5	183.1
	July	182.6	182.5
	April	179.6	179.0
	January	175.3	173.8

SOURCE: U. S. Department of Labor, Bureau of Labor Statistics
CPI Detailed Reports.

TABLE V
Gross Hours and Earnings of Production or Nonsupervisory Workers In Selected Manufacturing Industries

1972 SIC Code	Industry	Aver. weekly earnings				Aver. hourly earnings			
		Mar. 1980	Apr. 1980	Feb. 1981	Mar. 1981	Mar. 1980	Apr. 1980	Feb. 1981	Mar. 1981
	MACHINERY, EXCEPT ELECTRICAL—Continued	$371.87	$367.38	$412.78	$420.97	$9.32	$9.42	$10.53	$10.42
3531	Construction machinery	357.81	351.50	380.64	392.28	8.36	8.29	9.15	9.34
3532	Mining machinery	332.21	343.87	398.16	399.42	7.78	7.96	8.77	8.74
3533	Oil field machinery	301.67	304.78	310.57	310.90	7.34	7.47	8.13	8.16
3535	Conveyers and conveying equipment	297.35	297.92	311.81	312.86	7.49	7.60	8.12	8.19
3537	Industrial trucks and tractors	345.53	340.80	364.04	369.64	7.98	8.00	8.73	8.78
354	Metalworking machinery	364.52	360.86	382.30	385.37	8.21	8.22	8.87	8.90
3541	Machine tools, metal cutting types	361.44	344.87	355.69	359.70	8.29	8.31	8.87	8.97
3542	Machine tools, metal forming types	373.20	368.94	395.93	403.26	8.54	8.56	9.36	9.40
3544	Special dies, tools, jigs, and fixtures	310.98	308.59	324.72	333.98	7.30	7.33	7.92	7.99
3545	Machine tool accessories	251.07	246.41	271.05	270.78	6.23	6.27	6.95	7.07
3546	Power driven hand tools	304.41	302.32	327.54	330.79	7.30	7.32	7.95	7.99
355	Special industry machinery	316.83	314.24	341.02	341.38	7.69	7.74	8.44	8.45
3551	Food products machinery	248.63	241.80	258.32	261.53	6.02	6.00	6.41	6.41
3552	Textile machinery	323.36	318.42	350.96	357.73	7.52	7.51	8.20	8.30
3555	Printing trades machinery	319.66	318.61	343.92	349.79	7.74	7.79	8.45	8.49
356	General industrial machinery	318.06	312.73	344.06	350.06	7.72	7.76	8.58	8.58
3561	Pumps and pumping equipment	332.59	328.34	354.48	360.38	7.90	7.95	8.40	8.56
3562	Ball and roller bearings	338.13	343.48	370.86	374.36	8.07	8.12	8.83	8.85
3563	Air and gas compressors	289.64	288.56	304.55	315.46	7.03	7.09	7.71	7.77
3564	Blowers and fans	363.32	366.72	392.18	394.80	8.63	8.69	9.36	9.40
3566	Speed changers, drives, and gears	301.73	298.22	335.76	331.29	7.45	7.40	8.27	8.18
3568	Power transmission equipment, nec	274.07	267.15	295.39	296.12	6.51	6.58	7.24	7.24
357	Office and computing machines	278.38	271.26	292.54	293.25	6.55	6.60	7.17	7.17
3573	Electronic computing equipment	280.50	278.48	313.18	316.37	7.03	7.05	7.81	7.87
358	Refrigeration and service machinery	286.08	285.05	322.80	323.21	7.17	7.18	8.01	8.06
3585	Refrigeration and heating equipment	312.71	313.18	336.13	344.01	7.59	7.62	8.32	8.37
359	Misc. machinery, except electrical	346.28	356.53	394.42	397.36	8.55	8.76	9.91	9.86
3592	Carburetors, pistons, rings, valves	307.19	306.12	326.03	334.54	7.42	7.43	8.05	8.12
3599	Machinery, except electrical, nec								
36	**ELECTRIC AND ELECTRONIC EQUIPMENT**	271.20	268.88	295.02	301.10	6.78	6.79	7.45	7.49
361	Electric distributing equipment	271.48	272.52	292.70	295.26	6.77	6.83	7.41	7.40
3612	Transformers	266.38	266.67	288.55	298.98	6.61	6.65	7.25	7.31
3613	Switchgear and switchboard apparatus	275.71	276.71	295.93	292.47	6.91	6.97	7.53	7.48
362	Electrical industrial apparatus	280.42	278.18	311.25	315.24	6.89	6.92	7.61	7.67
3621	Motors and generators	280.98	277.26	312.94	319.61	6.87	6.88	7.67	7.72
3622	Industrial controls	276.29	276.61	296.40	299.09	6.95	6.95	7.41	7.44
363	Household appliances	266.66	261.29	292.55	301.72	6.82	6.84	7.54	7.60
3632	Household refrigerators and freezers	277.13	281.20	336.48	352.97	7.49	7.60	8.54	8.63
3633	Household laundry equipment	319.60	314.50	344.27	343.49	8.01	8.19	8.85	8.83
3634	Electric housewares and fans	217.06	211.07	231.33	238.58	5.58	5.54	6.04	6.04
364	Electric lighting and wiring equipment	249.55	247.27	271.66	278.88	6.26	6.26	6.86	6.92
3641	Electric lamps	276.58	278.70	304.17	306.43	6.88	6.95	7.72	7.68
3643	Current-carrying wiring devices	240.38	239.79	261.30	271.26	5.95	5.95	6.50	6.60
3644	Noncurrent-carrying wiring devices	256.31	253.62	288.35	293.53	6.44	6.47	7.05	7.09
3645	Residential lighting fixtures	177.97	184.73	209.72	213.10	4.81	4.90	5.49	5.45
365	Radio and TV receiving equipment	243.90	238.39	255.35	277.29	6.27	6.29	6.92	7.11
3651	Radio and TV receiving sets	253.49	248.52	266.35	285.25	6.55	6.54	7.16	7.39
366	Communication equipment	319.80	315.12	342.63	345.91	7.80	7.80	8.46	8.52
3661	Telephone and telegraph apparatus	331.25	322.80	357.82	356.06	8.04	8.01	8.77	8.77
3662	Radio and TV communication equipment	311.25	307.85	331.67	338.60	7.61	7.62	8.23	8.34
367	Electronic components and accessories	234.02	236.61	254.52	257.26	5.88	5.93	6.46	6.48
3671-3	Electronic tubes	310.73	323.64	327.95	331.27	7.26	7.44	7.96	8.06
3674	Semiconductors and related devices	271.06	269.73	295.73	293.86	6.64	6.66	7.32	7.31
3679	Electronic components, nec	218.28	220.25	235.38	239.18	5.54	5.59	6.02	6.04
369	Misc. electrical equipment and supplies	303.38	302.24	331.96	342.10	7.70	7.73	8.49	8.51
3691	Storage batteries	285.34	285.38	322.37	321.40	7.45	7.61	8.33	8.22
3694	Engine electrical equipment	337.26	335.62	362.70	380.33	8.67	8.65	9.47	9.58
37	**TRANSPORTATION EQUIPMENT**	365.22	359.79	398.59	414.70	9.04	9.04	9.94	10.09
371	Motor vehicles and equipment	378.58	366.70	419.36	444.29	9.56	9.50	10.59	10.81
3711	Motor vehicles and car bodies	401.95	393.78	461.38	490.69	10.28	10.39	11.77	11.91
3713	Truck and bus bodies	305.36	298.24	331.63	337.05	7.87	7.89	8.46	8.49
3714	Motor vehicle parts and accessories	374.79	362.48	408.83	429.73	9.30	9.20	10.17	10.38
3715,6	Truck trailers and motor homes	250.14	258.02	259.56	273.26	6.60	6.79	7.21	7.21
372	Aircraft and parts **	375.16	372.67	412.93	416.17	8.89	8.98	9.95	9.98
3721	Aircraft **	383.64	383.64	430.76	434.30	9.20	9.38	10.43	10.44
3724	Aircraft engines and engine parts	386.62	376.74	409.63	412.49	9.14	9.10	10.04	10.11
3728	Aircraft equipment, nec	346.09	346.25	378.75	383.56	8.03	8.09	8.87	8.92
373	Ship and boat building and repairing	322.36	326.03	345.14	363.85	7.94	8.05	8.65	8.81
3731	Shipbuilding and repairing	339.44	342.31	359.68	-	8.34	8.39	9.06	-
3732	Boat building and repairing	263.90	264.77	291.51	294.58	6.50	6.72	7.18	7.22
374	Railroad equipment	376.89	378.46	400.82	410.34	9.59	9.63	10.66	10.77

SOURCE: U. S. Department of Labor, *Employment and Earnings*, Vol. 28, No. 5 (May, 1981), p. 78.

CONTRACT BETWEEN KUB INDUSTRIES AND LOCAL 305
OF THE INTERNATIONAL UNION

AGREEMENT

This Agreement dated May 1, 1980, is entered into between KUB Industries, hereinafter referred to as the "Company," and Local 305 of the International Union, hereinafter referred to as the "Union."

Article I Purpose and Scope

It is the purpose of the parties hereto to give recognition to the mutual desire for industrial and economic harmony through the orderly and expeditious adjudication of all matters pertaining to wages, hours of work, pensions, insurance, working conditions, and other conditions of employment.

Article II Recognition

  section A -- The Company recognizes the Union as sole collective bargaining agent in the matter of wages, hours of work, pensions, insurance, working conditions, and other conditions of employment for all production and maintenance employees excluding office, professional, supervisory, and guard personnel as defined in the National Labor Relations Act.

  section B -- The Union agrees that members employed by the Company will work for the Company under the provisions set forth in this agreement. The Company and Union agree that all employees (as defined in section A of this article) employed since May 1, 1979 will become and remain members in good standing of the union within 30 days of their employment or within 30 days of the effective date of this contract, whichever comes later. The Company agrees that all employees (as defined in section A of this article) will be required as a condition of employment to remit to the Union the regular monthly dues of the Union. The Union, however, will be solely responsible for collecting such dues.

Article III Work Stoppages

  section A -- During the life of this Agreement, the Union agrees there shall be no strikes, slow downs, or work stoppages for any cause whatsoever. The Company agrees that there shall be no lockout for any cause whatsoever. The Company and Union agree to adjust all disputes through the grievance procedures set forth in this Agreement. The Union agrees to undertake in good faith the inducement of any employee engaged in a strike, slow-down, or work stoppage to return to work.

section B -- It is agreed that any strike, slow down, or work stoppage on the part of the Union or a lockout on the part of the Company shall be a violation of this Agreement, and that under no circumstances will there be discussion of disputes or grievances while such work interruption is in effect.

Article IV Hours of Work

section A -- The regular work week shall consist of five eight-hour work days. The factory shift hours shall be from (1) 7:00 AM to 3:00 PM, and (2) 3:00 P.M. to 11:00 P.M. Workers in the second shift will receive an 18 cent per hour premium. The day will include a thirty-minute lunch break with pay scheduled for the middle of the work period. In addition, each worker will receive a fifteen-minute coffee break in the morning and afternoon.

section B -- All work performed in excess of the normal eight-hour day at the request of management will be considered overtime and subject to a 50% premium based on the hourly wage rate. All work performed in excess of the forty-hour week at the request of management will be considered overtime and subject to a 50% premium based on the hourly wage rate.

section C -- All work performed on the following holidays will be subject to a 100% premium based on the hourly wage rate: New Years Day, President's Day, Memorial Day, Independence Day, Labor Day, Thanksgiving Day, and Christmas Day.

section D -- Each employee shall receive pay for each of the holidays (stated in section C) not worked provided: (1) he has been employed for not less than 30 days, (2) he worked his last scheduled day prior to the holiday and his first scheduled day following the holiday (unless permission has been granted to miss such a day), (3) he shall not have been on disciplinary suspension at time of holiday. The rate of pay for such holidays shall be the average straight time hourly wage for eight hours as appropriate for each employee.

Article V Wages

section A -- Wages shall be paid each Friday for the work performed the previous week, except when such payday falls on a holiday when checks will be available the day immediately prior.

section B -- The wage classification and conditions in effect in the plant at the signing of this agreement shall continue in effect during the life of this agreement and shall not be arbitrable.

section C -- The wage schedule in effect prior to contract settlement will be increased 25 cents per hour per worker.

section D -- The Company shall have the right to establish wage rates for new work or a change in process of manufacture. The Union may, within 5 days, object to such wage rates through the established grievance procedure.

Article VI Vacations

section A -- Employees shall be eligible for vacations with pay based upon the following schedule

(continuous service)	1 year (less than 5 yrs.) 5 years (less than 10 yrs.) 10 years (or more)	1 week 2 weeks 3 weeks	(vacation with pay)

section B -- Vacation pay for hourly workers shall be computed upon his or her average weekly pay for the month prior to said vacation. Payment will be made on the payday immediately prior to the beginning of the vacation period.

section C -- Any employee entering the Armed Forces shall receive, at time of leaving, his accumulated vacation pay computed at the rate of 1/12th of full vacation pay for each month or part of a month worked during that calendar year.
Any employee returning to the Company within 90 days of discharge from the Armed Forces shall after 60 days be eligible for full vacation pay at vacation time. However, said employees shall not receive intervening vacation pay.

Article VII   Grievances

section A -- The procedure set forth herein shall constitute the sole recourse with respect to any claim by an employee. Grievances shall consist only of disputes about wages, hours of work, and working conditions as provided in this Agreement.

section B -- (1) Grievances shall first be taken up by the department steward (an individual selected by the department) in an informal manner with the department foreman.

(2) If not adjusted, the complaint shall be reduced to writing and shall then constitute a formal grievance. The grievance shall then be submitted to the plant superintendent. If not settled with the superintendent, the grievance shall be submitted to a grievance committee composed of the General Manager, the Union President, and one additional person designated by each of them. This committee shall have authority to settle the grievance or refer the matter to arbitration.

Article VIII   Arbitration

section A -- Disputes and grievances unsettled through the grievance procedure may be submitted to arbitration as provided. The cost of such arbitration shall be borne by the company.

section B -- The Company and Union shall, within one calendar week from the receipt of an arbitration request, contact the Director of the Federal Mediation and Conciliation Service for a list of five arbitrators from which the Company and Union shall choose one. If the Company and Union fail to choose an arbitrator within one week, the Director of the Federal Mediation and Conciliation Service shall be notified to appoint an arbitrator. Any decision by the arbitrator shall be final and binding.

Article IX   Seniority

section A -- Probationary employees shall consist of those employees employed by the Company for a period less than thirty days.

section B -- Layoffs shall be made in the order of Company service beginning with the least. Recalls shall be made in the order of Company service beginning with the greatest.

section C -- An employee whose services are terminated either voluntarily or involuntarily shall lose all seniority rights.

section D -- Seniority shall consist of departmental seniority for actions within the department and Company seniority for actions between various departments or on a Company-wide basis.

Article X   Management

Section A -- All rights of the Company existing before the execution of this Agreement are retained by the Company, except as expressly modified by this Agreement.

section B -- The rights of section A above include, but are not limited by, the following: the general and overall management of the business and property, the direction of the work force including the right to hire, promote, demote, transfer, lay off, suspend, and discharge, and to require employees to observe rules and regulations.

section C -- The Company reserves the right to determine work standards, subcontracting practices, and the introduction of new processes.

section D -- The Company reserves the right to determine the type and amount of products manufactured, production standards, work schedules, materials used, and the number and starting times of shifts to be worked.

section E -- The Company shall be the sole determinant of the exercise of the rights in sections B and D and these shall therefore not be subject to the grievance procedure.

Article XI   Insurance and Pension Plans

section A -- The Company agrees to maintain in effect a group medical insurance plan for all employees so long as they remain on the Company's payroll. The cost of the premium shall be 60 percent payable by the company and 40 percent payable by the employee, whose share shall be payable by payroll deduction.

section B -- The Company shall maintain the existing, joint contributory pension plan. Details of the plan shall be made available by the Company to each employee.

Article XII

Amendments to this Agreement may be made at any time during the Agreement's life by mutual consent of the parties. The Amendments shall become a part of the Agreement and shall terminate at the same time as the original Agreement.

Article XIII

This Agreement shall continue in full force and effect for a period of one year at which time either party may announce its intention to terminate said Agreement within a period of not less than sixty days prior to expiration of the Agreement.

PLAYERS' ROLES

On the following pages is a set of role profiles, one of which will be assigned to you by either your instructor or your team members. In order to maximize the benefit of this simulation, it is important that you attempt to project yourself into your assigned role and, to the extent possible, identify with the views expressed in that profile. While you should not see the completed role profiles for the members of the opposing team, you should review all the completed profiles for your team. On the basis of your team's organization, you should complete the job description at the bottom of your assigned role profile.

UNION TEAM - LOCAL 305

a.   Field Representative - International Union

b.   President - Local 305

c.   Vice President - Local 305

d.   Treasurer - Local 305

e.   Chief Plant Steward - Local 305

MANAGEMENT TEAM

a.   Director - Corporate Industrial Relations

b.   Director - Financial Operations

c.   Director - Operations Management

d.   Manager - Organizational Development

e.   Manager - Compensation

DIRECTOR - CORPORATE INDUSTRIAL RELATIONS

You started with KUB Industries in 1964, and were one of the original employees to buy stock in the company. Prior to joining KUB, you were an Industrial Engineer with two years of college. When you started with the company, you knew everyone's name and were instrumental in establishing many of the outside social activities at KUB - the softball team, bowling team, etc. During the years, you have been guided by your personal philosophy of wanting to keep the employees happy at KUB so that it was a good place to work. From the time you started until 1970, you were the Personnel Department at KUB. When the 1970 strike occurred, you were deeply upset by the existence of the Union. You still haven't accepted the Union in KUB Industries.

Since 1970, you have progressed to your present position where you are responsible for all aspects of Labor Relations. Included in your functions are employer relations, training, industrial relations, organizational planning, job evaluation, wage administration (salaried and hourly), and public relations. You have been extremely active in community and professional organizations.

In the forthcoming negotiations, you realize the need for higher wages for the employees, but you are also concerned about rising costs through inflation. In addition, you have been concerned about the potential effects of environmental activities and discontinuities in fuel supply in regard to the company's major customer - the auto industry.

You also recognize the need for tighter job and cost controls stressed by the Operations Department. You see the necessity for job evaluation, mandatory overtime, and the development of standards. In addition, you have a difficult time understanding the demands of your employees. You feel that the fringe benefits package and wages make KUB a good place to work. You feel the need for more discipline within the workforce.

Overall, you are responsible for developing and coordinating management's strategy and demands for the forthcoming negotiation.

Based upon the organization of your bargaining team, the specific responsibilities of the Director - Corporate Industrial Relations include the following:

DIRECTOR - FINANCIAL OPERATIONS

You are responsible for the financial expenditures and allocations of resources within the firm. In addition, you have the responsibility for the financial representation of the firm to the stockholders, banks, and other financial institutions. You are a C.P.A. Your cost accounting background in the auto industry was a major factor in your recent hire into KUB Industries.

Since this is your first negotiation with KUB, you are determined to keep the cost structure in line with other companies in the same industry and area. You are considered to have a high degree of expertise in the development of cost control procedures. Your prior experience has strengthened your determination in advocating a "hard line" toward union activities. Wage levels, benefit packages, and similar items must be contingent upon increased productivity and cost consciousness. You are concerned with the potential dissatisfaction of stockholders should company profits decrease.

Based upon the organization of your bargaining team, the specific responsibilities of the Director - Financial Operations include the following:

DIRECTOR - OPERATIONS MANAGEMENT

As Director of Operations Management, you are responsible for the production facilities at KUB. Prior to joining KUB in 1976, you were a Production Supervisor in the auto industry. In this job, you gained a reputation as a tough, driving, production-centered manager.

Your main concern in the Production area centers around increasing productivity, keeping quality at a high level, and reducing costs. Due to this concern, you have been active in promoting subcontracting as a means to insure component quality and meet peak periods of demand without having to hire and train new employees. You are concerned about the abilities and motivation of the people whom you feel that you are being forced to hire.

You are primarily concerned about the retention of management rights in the forthcoming negotiation. You do not want the company to bargain away any item that may place restrictions on your department's productivity efforts. You do not want the union to go on strike because you realize the production costs involved. At the same time, you want the employees to get higher wages so that you do not lose any of your trained employees-- especially skilled employees--to another company.

You agree with the concept that a person should be promoted on the basis of merit and ability. You are against the seniority system and strongly oppose affirmative action programs. You have no long-term acquaintances with KUB since you are a relative newcomer to the organization. You are somewhat apprehensive of staff people and college graduates. You prefer to identify with employees who get ahead through drive and ambition.

Your greatest areas of concern in the forthcoming negotiations are costs and efficiency of operation.

Based upon the organization of your bargaining team, the specific responsibilities of the Director - Operations Management include the following:

MANAGER - ORGANIZATION DEVELOPMENT

As O.D. Manager, you report to the Director of Industrial Relations. You were recently hired after graduation from a small liberal arts college; since you are receiving Veterans' benefits, you are continuing your education at night at Paine University. During your course of studies for the Master's Degree in Social Work, you strengthened your commitment to a high degree of social concern for business.

Your specific responsibilities include training and development and employee guidance and counseling. You have been attempting to persuade line management to engage in job humanization in order to make jobs more meaningful to the employees. You are concerned that the other negotiators are pressing for production standards, mandatory overtime, and job evaluation. You firmly believe that this traditional approach alienates the employees. You identify heavily with the interests of the younger and minority employees and believe that KUB should make up for their alleged past discriminatory practices.

The Industrial Relations Director has placed you on the negotiating team in order to gain practical experience, to take care of some of the detailed analytical work, and to be his "pulse" for how the younger employees would react to the negotiated items. However, you feel that this may be the only opportunity for you to make a meaningful input into the KUB Industries negotiations.

Based upon the organization of your bargaining team, the specific responsibilities of the Manager - Organization Development include the following:

MANAGER - COMPENSATION

As Manager of Compensation you report directly to the Director of Industrial Relations. While you have served in this capacity for a couple of years with a somewhat smaller non-union firm, you are one of the newer members of the KUB management team. You were hired at a rather attractive salary because of your technical knowledge of wage and salary administration. You are quite ambitious and take pride in your professional approach to compensation problems.

Since this is the first time you will have been involved in collective bargaining, you are looking forward to this learning experience. At the same time, you see this as a good opportunity to impress your boss and other members of the negotiating team with your expertise in all phases of wages and fringe benefits.

Based upon the organization of your bargaining team, the specific responsibilities of the Manager of Compensation include the following:

You are a long-time employee of KUB Industries, having started with KUB in 1966. After several years, you became an active proponent of unionization in KUB Industries, culminating in your leadership in the 1970 strike. Since that time, you have been an elected official in Local 305. You have worked diligently for the union and devoted many long hours to local and international union activities. You are known as a tough bargainer who is prone to reward his friends and punish his enemies. Since becoming President of Local 305 in 1975, you have become politically astute.

Until recently, your leadership of the union has been unquestioned. You have been the major force in setting local union policy and negotiation strategy. Anyone who disagreed with your position became quickly discouraged.

Your major support in the union comes from the long-term employees. Informally, you seek advice and information from the other members of the "70 Fraternity"--the group of employees that still remain in KUB from the early organizing days and strike of 1970. Often, the group gets together and talks about "the good old days." Since you are a skilled employee, another major area of support comes from the skilled employees in KUB.

Therefore, you are a long-time advocate of increased benefits for the older and skilled employees. Your bargaining strategy places heavy emphasis on seniority rights, pension plans, protection from layoff, insurance, increased salary differentials for skilled employees, and other longevity benefits. You plan to take good care of this group during the forthcoming negotiations.

You cannot understand the demands of younger employees. Although the international union has advocated increased participation in local activities, you believe that they "should wait their turn since we know what's best for 'em."

Based upon the organization of your bargaining team, the specific responsibilities of the Local President include the following:

FIELD REPRESENTATIVE - INTERNATIONAL UNION

You have been affiliated with the International Union for 20 years, progressing through the ranks to your present position. You started as an elected steward in KUB Industries in 1970 and became affiliated as a full-time staff member with IU in 1975. Your peers consider you to be a professional in the labor field. Your strong points include an ability to reconcile diverse issues at the bargaining table as well as being able to conduct yourself in moderation. You are an experienced and skilled negotiator and you are able to effectively organize your bargaining team, strategy, and agenda.

Your role is extremely essential to the welfare and survival of the local union's affiliation with the International. One of your main functions is to serve as a liaison between the local and international union. In doing so, you are responsible for the enforcement of the international union's policies and guidelines in relation to issues which supersede the interests of the local union. Some of these issues entail check-off, union security issues, salary alignments, and reconciliation of internal conflict issues. You are known for your ability to reconcile diverse issues and viewpoints within the union. Usually, you do not take sides with any particular faction of the union's membership.

Recently, one of your main functions has been to resist the pressures of local union members who desire to have the Local split away from the International. Overall, you attempt to secure the best contract available for the local without endangering the on-going profitability and survival of the firm. You are a resource as to what is happening with other companies in the industry.

Based upon the organization of your bargaining team, the specific responsibilities of the Field Representative - International Union include the following:

You are a younger employee of KUB, recently elected as Vice President. After two years of college, you had enlisted and spent three years in the army. Your college experience provided you with technical knowledge of labor relations, since this was your major field. Your military experience changed your outlook on life on many issues. After your discharge, you were married. You decided to find a job and go to college at night rather than go back full-time.

At work, you became associated with a militant splinter-group, KUBRUM (KUB Revolution-ary Union Movement). Many of the members of this group were also continuing their education on a part-time basis. Your leadership experience in the military enabled you to assume a leadership position among the younger employees. Your active advocacy of the rights of younger and minority employees enabled you to be elected to your present position as Local Vice-President.

The younger employees in KUB want preferential treatment in the forthcoming negotiations. They feel that the local union's leadership has not taken care of the interests of younger employees. If they do not receive their demands, there is increasing pressure to disaffiliate with the International and join a more militant national union. They are increasingly concerned about what inflation is doing to their purchasing power and want a substantial salary increase as well as some additional protection. An escalator clause has been mentioned. The younger employees also want more attention paid to ability rather than seniority.

The younger and minority employees feel that "the mortgage is due," and have elected you to press for their demands. They have become frustrated at the policies of the older union leaders.

Based upon the organization of your bargaining team, the specific responsibilities of the Vice President - Local 305 include the following:

You are the financial analyst for the local union. You are a long-term employee of KUB and belong to the "70 Fraternity"--a group of employees who worked at KUB during the formation of the local and the 1970 strike. At that time, you became Treasurer and your interest in financial matters prompted you to take a number of related courses at a local community college. Although you are a long-term employee, you are sympathetic to the demands of the younger and minority employees. You are concerned with avoiding a split within the union. Thus, you are primarily concerned with developing a set of demands which would be the best overall package for all the employees.

You are primarily responsible for developing a total wage and benefit set of demands which would be best for the employees. However, you realize that the company does not have the financial resources of many of the larger firms in the Detroit area. You would want to balance your demands with your concern for the survival of the firm. Recent events--such as the fuel shortage and trend toward compact cars--have caused you to reflect on the implications for the forthcoming negotiations.

You are in the position to know that the financial reserves of the local cannot support a strike of any long duration. You are not certain if the International Union would financially support striking employees.

Based upon the organization of your bargaining team, the specific responsibilities of the Treasurer include the following:

As a newer member of Local 305 at KUB Industries, you have never really had an active voice in the Union nor has anyone ever regarded you as a leader within the organization. You were recently elected as Chief Plant Steward as a compromise candidate. No one really expects you to function as an active Chief Steward.

Therefore, you are determined to prove to everyone that you are going to be a major force in the Local. You are going to show everyone that you are equal to the job requirements and entitled to long-overdue respect. Since this is the first time you will be involved in contract negotiations, you view this as an excellent opportunity to impress the Union members with your negotiating expertise.

Since everyone on the bargaining team regards you as an interim candidate, you have no specific duties assigned to you. However, you are determined to analyze the present situation and the rules of the other negotiators in order to gain expertise in the areas not specifically covered by them.

Based upon your analysis of the situation and the organization of your bargaining team, the specific duties of the Chief Plant Steward include the following:

APPENDIX: FORMS

FORM A – STRATEGY FORMAT
(One Copy to Instructor – One Copy Retained)

ITEM DEMANDED	DEMAND PRIORITY	LOWEST ACCEPTABLE OFFER	EXPECTATION	INITIAL DEMAND*

*OR CONTRACT CHANGE

FORM B - BARGAINING AGENDA
(2 Copies to be Presented to Opposing Team)

ITEM DEMANDED

INITIAL DEMAND

FORM C – ARGUMENTATION SEQUENCE
(For Use of Team)

ITEM DEMANDED	DEMAND PRIORITY	ORDER OF PRESENTATION	RESOURCE PERSON	ARGUMENTS FOR DEMAND

37

FORM D – REBUTTAL SCHEDULE

ANTICIPATED DEMAND BY OPPONENTS	INITIAL ESTIMATED DEMAND	ESTIMATED PRIORITY	RESOURCE PERSON	ARGUMENTS AGAINST DEMAND

FORM E

Name Card

(Each player should complete and place in front during negotiations. Fold and place upright.)

TITLE:

NAME:

FORM F – NEGOTIATION SUMMARY

ITEM #	ITEM	ESSENTIAL FEATURES OF AGREEMENT

43

FORM G

Evaluation of Opposing Team
(to be given to instructor)

Team: #_____   Evaluated by Team: #_____

Strong points of opponents:

Weak points of opponents:

REPORT OF CONTRACT NEGOTIATION AUDIT
TEAM_____'S AUDIT OF TEAM_____

The following questions are to be used as a guideline in evaluating the performance of the team that you audited.

1. Quantitative ($) costs of the contract.

2. Qualitative costs of the contract   (i.e., loss of power by either side; rights previously had by the team which no longer are in their control, etc.).

3. How did this team meet or fail to meet their expectations?
    (Comparison of expectations (Form A) with actual contract;
    were the team's expectations realistic?)

4. How did each member of the team carry out his or her role description?
    What demands of the group that they represent show up in the final contract?

5. What are the strong points of the contract for this team?
    Weak points?

6. What are the likely sources of grievances under this contract?

7. What are the likely points for re-negotiation at the next contract negotiation? What provisions have the bargainings made for future issues?

8. Additional comments on the evaluation of the team's performance:

FORM I

CONTRACT NEGOTIATION AUDIT (Summary)

TEAM_____'S   AUDIT OF TEAM_____

Priority	Item Demanded (per form A)	Contract Clause	Initial Demand	Expectation	Actual Result

(Item not in Form A)

53

FORM J

KUBSIM: INDIVIDUAL APPRAISAL FORM

Your Name_____   Your Team_____

All information on this appraisal form will be held in absolute confidence. This form and its contents may not be communicated to any other class member.

Rank each member of your team in alphabetical order including yourself. For each of the items tested, rank each individual on a scale from 0 (lowest) to 10 (highest). This ranking indicates your appraisal of each individual's contribution to your team's performance per each item listed.

No two persons may receive the same rating on the same items!

Name							
1. Knowledge of KUBSIM rules and background							
2. Knowledge of overall collective bargaining material							
3. Research contribution – developed outside information							
4. Ability to carry out assigned role							
5. Contribution to team morale							
6. Attendance at team planning session							
7. Negotiation ability (with other team)							
8. Ability to plan for contingencies							
9. Ability to see the other team member's point of view							
10. Overall value to team							
TOTAL (of above)							

Additional information you may wish to add to aid in the evaluation process:

1896